Survive office politics

How to steer a course through minefields at work

A & C Black • London

First published in 2004 by
Bloomsbury Publishing Plc

Reprinted 2006 by A & C Black
38 Soho Square
London W1D 3HB

British Library Cataloguing in Publication Data
A CIP record for this book is available from the British Library.

ISBN 0–7136–8200–0

Design by Fiona Pike, Pike Design, Winchester
Typeset by RefineCatch Limited, Bungay, Suffolk
Printed by Graphycems, Spain

A & C Black uses paper produced with elemental chlorine-free pulp, harvested from managed sustainable forests.

Contents

How well do you handle office politics?

Answer the questions and work out your political profile, then read the guidance points.

When you started your job, how long did it take you to learn about the office politics?

a) 10 months b) 5 months c) 1 month

Complete the following statement 'You get ahead at work by . . . '

a) doing your job well, and doing it by the rules
b) putting the needs and goals of the team ahead of your own
c) watching your back and pushing hard to achieve personal goals

How often do you gossip?

a) Hardly ever b) Fairly regularly c) All the time!

How much does *who* you know count in your office?

a) I don't know. Everyone keeps to themselves.
b) Not much. I have to perform well and achieve high results to get rewards.
c) A lot. Getting on well with my managers and doing a favour or two for some people will get me a long way.

How well do you get on with your boss?

a) OK. I don't really have much contact with him/her.
b) Very well. We complement each other.
c) Terribly – it's a complete clash of personalities.

How many trusted allies do you have at work?

a) 1 to 3 b) 4 to 7 c) 8 or more

Do you feel able to 'be yourself' in the office?

a) No b) Not completely c) Yes

How often do you socialise with colleagues?

a) Very seldom b) Fairly regularly c) Very regularly

To what extent do you 'network'?

a) Not at all. I feel awkward about 'using' people.
b) Fairly regularly. It depends if I have a definite need and can see an opportunity.
c) Whenever I can, in case I ever need a favour.

How often do office politics get in the way of work?

a) Never b) Sometimes c) Regularly

How often do you think about non-verbal ways of communicating?

a) Non-*what*?
b) Quite often. Especially if I'm dealing with difficult people and think it might help to build rapport.
c) All the time. I try to copy the way people talk and behave.

a = 1, b = 2, and c = 3. Now add up your scores.

12–19: Either you work in an extremely relaxed and open work culture, or you're unwilling to get involved in office politics. Chapters **1** and **2** argue that it's important to accept that politics are necessary and unavoidable, and that a certain amount of political nous can be healthy, helping you to get ahead in your career and contribute to the success of the organisation—it's all about effective communication. Pay attention to non-verbal signs (chapter **4**), and start making a stronger impression on colleagues (chapter **5**).

20–27: You appear to have a healthy attitude towards the political environment at work, but be wary of being drawn into the culture of gossiping that exists in most offices—don't be tempted into politicking! Get advice on how to advance your career by successful networking (chapter **6)** and by making a great impression on colleagues and managers (chapter **5**).

28–36: You're at risk of becoming unhealthily embroiled in office politics. Too much gossip is dangerous and unprofessional, and can lose you friends—and your job. Instead of getting involved in negative political manoeuvring, try to expose it. If a difficult relationship with your boss is making office life hard, read chapter **3**. Sometimes relationships with colleagues can turn sour; read chapter **7** for advice on managing office romances, and chapters **4** and **5** to help polish your influencing and communication skills. There's advice on dealing with the politics of meetings in chapter **8**.

1 Understanding internal politics

by Kathleen Kelley Reardon
Professor of Management and Organisation at the University of Southern California Marshall School of Business

Many of the hurdles managers must face and overcome have little to do with technical competence. Rather, they have to do with politics. Internal politics is a fact of life in organisations, yet many managers and CEOs will tell you their success is largely due to allowing 'no politics' in their firms. They'll regale you with stories of how they use and encourage 'people skills' to create a desired environment and accomplish organisational goals. What they're really talking about is how they use politics.

Step one: Accept that politics is a part of office life

In common vernacular, 'politics' is used to describe what people do to influence decision-makers, accomplish hidden agendas, and surreptitiously advance their careers, often to the detriment of others. But politics is not always so sinister.

By its very nature, politics involves going outside usual, formally sanctioned channels to accomplish objectives. However, it doesn't have to be done in a secretive manner and the results can often benefit everyone involved. When used to influence people in the service of valid company goals, politics becomes a positive tool indeed. The team leader who makes valuable connections with people who can advance the team's efforts is acting politically.

Given two competent people, the one who has political savvy, agility in the use of power, and the ability to influence others is more likely to succeed as a senior manager. Indeed, to the successful senior manager in a competitive organisation, day-to-day life *is* politics. That's why smart business people think like Caroline Nahas, managing director of Korn Ferry International, Southern California. To be politically astute, you need to 'read where the trend lines are' and 'be ahead of the game'.

Of course, politics is not always positive. Sometimes, people must defend themselves from political manoeuvring. When surrounded or targeted by colleagues playing underhand political games, job survival may require one to act similarly. In organisations where bias or favouritism dictate who gets key assignments and promotions, political manoeuvring is required to get into the loop.

In short, the astute employee or manager must understand how politics functions in organisations in order to advance his or her and the firm's own goals.

Step two: Assess how political your workplace is

The first step in acquiring political acumen is learning to identify the kind of political organisation you're working in. Without this knowledge, you'll be operating in the dark, wondering why opportunities were lost. There are four primary levels of political arena—minimal, moderate, highly political, and pathologically political—and they often co-exist inside a large organisation.

1 Minimally politicised

The atmosphere is amicable. Conflicts rarely occur and don't usually last long. The atmosphere is comradely—there's an absence of in-groups and out-groups, and one person's gain isn't seen as another's loss.

Rules may be bent and favours granted, but people treat each other with regard and rarely resort to underhand political means. These are excellent environments for people uncomfortable with aggressive politics. Unfortunately, such organisations are more the exception than the rule.

2 Moderately politicised

These types of organisation operate on commonly understood and formally sanctioned rules. They often include smaller, fast-moving firms and large ones focused on organisational agility. Where customer focus, results, teamwork, and interpersonal trust are priorities, politics is rarely destructive, and often focuses on surfacing worthwhile ideas.

Achieving objectives via unsanctioned methods isn't unusual, but tends to be subtle and deniable. When conflicts get out of hand, managers will invoke sanctioned rules or common principles for resolution.

As a manager, however, when such an arena becomes dysfunctional, you will see considerable denial before unspoken political rules surface to the point where you can identify and address them constructively.

3 Highly politicised

Conflict is pervasive in this kind of culture. Instead of applying formal rules consistently, combatants only invoke them when convenient. In-groups and out-groups are clearly defined. Few people dare to communicate directly with senior managers. 'Who' is more important than 'what' you know, and work is often highly stressful, especially for those in out-groups.

When there's conflict, people rely on aggressive political methods and involve others in the dispute. Highly political organisations are usually incapable of resolving conflicts constructively. They place blame and don't tolerate losers. Such quick fixes rarely alter the dysfunctional pattern.

4 Pathologically politicised

These organisations are often on the verge of self-destruction. Productivity is suboptimal and information massaging is prevalent. People distrust each other, interactions are often fractious, and conflict is long-lasting and pervasive. People must circumvent formal procedures and structures to achieve objectives. They spend much time covering their backs.

Management uses a carrot-and-stick approach to control people. Subordinates are seen as stubborn, wilful—even stupid. In the classic *Harvard Business Review* article, 'Asinine Attitudes toward Motivation', Harry Levinson described this as the 'jackass fallacy'.

Step three: Recognise the signs of political pathology

To avoid political pathology, managers must recognise its encroachment. Here are five indicators that it's time to alter the political environment to save it from self-destruction.

- **Frequent flattery** of persons in power, coupled with abuse of people in weaker positions.
- **Information massaging**. No one says anything that might rock the boat, and the common means of communication is hint and innuendo.

- **Malicious gossip** and backstabbing are common, even where little overt conflict appears.
- **Cold indifference**, where no one is valued and everyone is dispensable, indicates the area has been systemically polluted by people in charge. Survival is based on obsequiousness, and getting others before they get you.
- **Fake left, go right**. People, even entire departments, purposely mislead others in order to look good when they fail. Teamwork is absent. Managers sacrifice subordinates' careers to avoid looking bad.

Step four: Match political style to political culture

A crucial step in learning to manage politics is identifying individual political styles. The mix of styles and their 'fit' with the predominant political arena exert considerable influence on goal achievement.

1 The purist

The least political are 'purists', who believe in getting ahead through hard work. They shun politics, and rely on following sanctioned rules to get things done. Purists are usually honest—sometimes naïvely so. They believe in getting ahead by doing their job well. Purists trust other people and prefer to work with those who do the same.

Behind-the-scenes grappling for power and prestige is not of interest, hence purists are best suited to minimally political climates and will struggle to survive in highly political or pathological arenas.

2 The team player

'Team players' believe you get ahead by working with others and using politics that advance the goals of the group. They rarely put their own individual career needs ahead of group needs. Team players prefer to operate according to a set of sanctioned rules, but will trade favours or engage in other relatively benign politics to achieve team goals. Focused on doing the job well and creating conditions for team member advancement, team players are best suited to moderately political environments.

3 The street fighter

An individualist, the 'street fighter' believes the best way to get ahead is via rough tactics. The street fighter relies more on subliminal politics than the purist and the team player, but is just as likely to invoke sanctioned rules when they serve personal goals.

Street fighters watch their backs, push hard to achieve personal goals, and are slow to trust others. They thrive on the 'cut and thrust' of business, enjoy intrigue, and derive gratification from working the system. The street fighter is comfortable in highly political arenas and can survive in pathological ones as well.

4 The manoeuvrer

The 'manoeuvrer' is also an individualist, one who believes in getting ahead by playing political games in a skilful, unobtrusive manner. Subtler than the street fighter, but uninhibited about using politics to advance personal objectives and favoured team objectives, manoeuvrers prefer to operate in a more covert and underhand way. They tend to look for ulterior motives in others, have little regard for sanctioned rules, and rely largely on subliminal politics.

These smooth operators are less committed to hard work than purists, and only operate as team players when it suits their agendas. People get in the way of a manoeuvrer at their own peril. The manoeuvrer is best suited to highly political and pathological arenas.

✔ Assess the arena prevalent in your division, and that of the larger organisation. Is it becoming highly political or pathological? If so, is this because opinion leaders are of the street fighter or manoeuvrer styles? There's nothing inherently wrong with street fighters and the occasional manoeuvrer may be an asset if he or she brings something valuable to the group. A predominance of these styles, however, can tip a division or company closer to pathology. And once an organisation finds itself in this situation, it can be extremely difficult to reverse. Familiarise yourself with political warning signs and take steps to stem the tide of political self-destruction.

Common mistakes

✗ Failing to understand or rejecting internal politics

Trying to pretend there is no such thing as internal politics or making no attempt to understand the political style of your organisation, particularly if you are a manager, is very risky. Politics is a reality in the workplace and, consequently, one must learn to survive and manage the conflicts that arise from political behaviour. The negative and positive effects reverberate on individual employees as well as the organisation as a whole. Remember that politics, in and of itself, is not bad if it works to serve company goals by making sure that the workplace is productive and that morale remains high.

✗ Not heeding the warning signs of political pathology until it's too late

A pathologically political work environment is ultimately a self-destructive one in which conflict and distrust flourish, and productivity, morale, and ultimately, the success of the company, are jeopardised. There are ways to detect when the political atmosphere is becoming unhealthily charged and ways to deal with this situation should it arise. Look out for signs of political pathology, such as excessive flattery, information massaging, and malicious gossip (see Step three). Chapter 2 offers solutions and advice for handling politics at work.

STEPS TO SUCCESS

- ✔ Advancing business and career goals often necessitates acting politically.
- ✔ Assess the degree to which your organisation is politicised. Is the atmosphere amicable or distrustful? Is the workforce productive, or does conflict prevent work being done?
- ✔ As a manager you need to identify the political style of your employees and then monitor them to see how they contribute to the dynamic and success of the organisation.
- ✔ Learn to recognise the signs of impending political pathology, such as malicious gossip, information massaging, lack of teamwork, and frequent flattery.
- ✔ To ensure career success and the achievement of goals, you need to match your individual political style—and those of your employees if you are a manager—to the firm's environment.
- ✔ Take steps to detoxify the workplace: communicate more openly and directly, invoke sanctioned rules or shared mores to resolve conflict, and emphasise solving problems over placing blame. Politics must never be allowed to degenerate into a self-destructive process.

Useful links

About.com:

http://careerplanning.about.com

monstertrak:

http://content.monstertrak.monster.com/resources/archive/onthejob/politics

totaljobs.com:

www.totaljobs.com

2 Handling office politics

Life would be wonderful if you could work in an office without worrying about other people and what they're up to. However, everyone has a network of relationships throughout the organisation, and if you don't handle those carefully, you could be heading for a career disaster.

You don't have to work somewhere long to work out whether or not it has a highly political culture, where *who* you know tends to matter more than *what* you know. Friendships and casual conversations take on a new significance—one wrong word to the wrong person could end up scuppering that promotion.

The context in which people have come to know each other is also important, as that can imply certain kinds of loyalty (or perceived obligations). Family, school, or social networks that intrude into professional territory can embroil people in all sorts of Machiavellian manoeuvrings that eventually create an overly politically-charged workplace. If you find yourself in this sort of minefield, this chapter offers advice on how to pick your way through and use politics in a positive way. It also

suggests ways for managers to avoid and discourage negative 'politicking'.

Step one: Watch for signs of office politics

Politics plays a part in all organisations; it's an inevitable effect of putting human beings together in some sort of hierarchical arrangement. Indicators of office politics are often fairly easy to pick up—just hang around near the kettle, water cooler, or canteen in any organisation.

✔ Listen out for clues about how the business works under the surface. Perhaps you might hear comments from people who have been passed over for promotion in favour of the recruiting manager's former golf partner.

✔ Watch out for those who succeed by publicly supporting their boss, or by ensuring that they are always in the right place at the right time. Such successes again indicate that hidden agendas may be at play.

TOP TIP

If you're already embroiled in a nasty political situation, it's important to go through the correct channels to avoid compromising yourself further. Explain what's happened to your supervisor or manager. If the situation involves your boss, you may

want to approach your human resources department (if you have one) to ask their advice about how to proceed.

Step two: Ensure your own survival

Self-preservation is always desirable, but don't use political dirty tricks to survive, whatever your level of responsibility—they'll only create new nightmares. If your organisation is rife with politics, you can survive by following some simple rules.

- ✔ Observe the organisation's political style without getting involved until you're sure that you know what is going on. You may have started to notice coincidences or inconsistencies. Bide your time and watch the process so that you can begin to understand what the patterns and motivations are.

- ✔ Keep your own counsel during this period and work according to your own values. Don't try to change your values to match those of the organisation; under pressure, your own values will reassert themselves forcefully. You can't please everyone all the time, so use your own integrity to make decisions.

- ✔ Build a network of trusted allies. During your observation phase you will have identified who these people could be. It's also a good idea to build a network outside the organisation to create options and opportunities for yourself. This will take the focus off work for a while and gives you time to reconfirm or realign your values.

TOP TIP

Male networks have controlled the power in businesses for hundreds of years and can seem impenetrable. If you're a woman in a man's world, you may find it helpful to find a mentor (male or female) inside or outside the business, who will champion you and look out for information and opportunities for you. Build your relationships carefully and find ways to contribute your skills and ideas that will be valued by your male colleagues. Don't let them take advantage of your talents, though; follow up and ask for feedback. In this way, you will build their respect and find a tenable position among them.

✔ Expose other people's politically-motivated behaviour. When colleagues say one thing and do another, or seem to be sabotaging your decisions or work relationships, use your assertiveness skills to challenge their motivation: 'You seem to be unhappy with the decisions I've made; would you like to discuss them?' They'll either have to deny your assertion or confront it, but at least the issue will be out in the open.

✔ Find a mentor with whom you can discuss your observations and concerns. You may gain a deeper understanding of the political processes at work and some insight into how you can manage these more effectively.

TOP TIP

If you're in a large organisation but want to avoid politics in your working life, you may find that a change of environment meets your needs. This doesn't necessarily mean a move out of the organisation entirely, but perhaps you could consider a move to a small-business unit or specialised department where there may be a different political culture. Smaller work units are very often structurally simpler and less political than large ones.

Step three: Discourage negative political behaviour

In any working environment, decision-making based on self-interested politics will encourage hypocrisy, double-dealing, cliques, and deception. These must be reined in if the business is to survive in the long term. Here are a few tips for those in managerial positions on how to create change and avoid potential nightmares:

- ✔ Give promotions to the candidates who've demonstrated a relevant track record of success. Conduct structured, formal interviews and consult with others affected by the decision. Match the successful candidate to the job description. Remember that although a good working relationship is necessary, the talents and values of the candidate don't have to match those of their new line manager exactly.

- ✔ Offer rewards and recognition solely for good performance, not in return for favours. All promotions or pay rises must be based on the individual's ability to reach or exceed the key performance indicators set during the performance review. Performance data should be available to those it concerns, with no hidden judgments or decisions.

- ✔ Communicate openly and transparently. Only unhealthy organisations hide information and spring unpleasant surprises on their employees. Communicate anything that affects your employees and their performance, including bad news, challenges, and initiatives for change.

- ✔ Introduce new initiatives, projects, and ideas on the basis of their value to the business, not on the basis of favouritism or possible personal benefit. Setting up a formal process for proposing new initiatives and tracing their evaluation and implementation will create confidence in an unbiased outcome.

✔ Don't be tempted to indulge in 'politicking', even when you can see an opportunity to benefit either yourself or the organisation as a whole. For example, you might want to offload a member of your team in order to attract someone you feel may perform more effectively. However, this is where the rot sets in. If you manage people on this basis, you'll destroy any trust your team has in you and their collective performance may deteriorate.

Common mistakes

✗ You misread a situation and wade in with an accusation of politicking

At best this reveals your naïvety, at worst your own politicking or neuroses. If you think a colleague is politically motivated, observe their behaviour until you're sure that you understand it. You may wish to share your thoughts with someone you trust or, if it serves a purpose, confront the situation. However, remember that sometimes the best option is to take a step back and just leave things alone.

✗ You build a network purely for your own ends

Some people try to short-circuit the path to promotion by cultivating what they believe to be essential relationships. However, there's a big difference between building professional networks and using your contacts shamelessly in a headlong pursuit of your own selfish ends. Remember that if you launch yourself into an early promotion without having developed the skills to be successful, you may be setting yourself up for a very public and career-damaging failure. Build your networks prudently and use them to help develop your skills and deliver new opportunities. It may take a little longer, but it will pay off in the end.

✗ You get involved in the politics too early

When you join a new organisation, try not to get embroiled in the politics at an early stage. Your newness in the business will allow you to ask naïve questions that will help you create a picture of the political environment. Keep your relationships open and friendly and build your network with a diverse range of people. Observe the patterns of relationships closely to see where the information lies and where the power sits. After a few months you'll probably have a fairly accurate idea of what's going on and you can then make your own decisions about the extent to which you should get involved in organisational politics.

✗ You communicate badly

Poor communication is probably the most common cause of a destructive political culture. In the absence of information or explanation, people will fill the gaps with speculation and rumour, which circulate around the office grapevine very fast. Clear communication, leaving people in no doubt about plans or decisions, helps protect an organisation from becoming a breeding ground for politics. Newsletters, bulletin boards on an intranet, and company-wide meetings are all useful vehicles for disseminating information, along with more local activities such as team meetings, departmental get-togethers, and personal briefings.

STEPS TO SUCCESS

- ✔ Listen out for signs of political machinations. Informal situations are often the most fruitful for this kind of research.
- ✔ Communicate openly and transparently in order to discourage gossip and encourage trust.
- ✔ Don't be tempted into negative politicking—it's unlikely to end well. Keep out of it and retain your integrity. Also try to dispel other people's politically-motivated behaviour by exposing it.
- ✔ Build a network of trusted allies and confidants, both inside and outside the organisation. If you can, find a mentor with whom you can discuss any concerns.
- ✔ If you must confront a political situation, go through formal channels so that your position isn't compromised further.
- ✔ Try not to get involved until you fully understand all aspects of the conflict.

Useful links

Doctor Job:

www.doctorjob.com

iVillage office politics:

www.ivillage.co.uk/workcareer

Guardian Jobs

http://jobs.guardian.co.uk

3 Coping with a difficult boss

Many people have a difficult or challenging relationship with their boss. Of all the difficult relationships you may have at work, this will probably be the trickiest and most stressful because of the inherent political dynamic of your relationship. It can be tempting to lay the blame for this unhappy type of situation at the boss's feet due to his or her unreasonable, negative, awkward, or unhelpful behaviour. Whether justified or not, the good news is that, as a significant party in the relationship, there is much you can do to end the bad boss nightmare.

Step one: Consider the impact on your own health and happiness

Rather than deal with the problem directly, many people are tempted to live with the difficulties of having a troublesome boss. Instead of addressing the problem, they brush it under the carpet by looking for ways of minimising the impact he or she has on their working lives. However, employing avoidance tactics or finding ways to offset the emotional damage can be time-consuming and stressful. Focusing on your own well-being may encourage you to tackle the issue rationally and try to reach an accommodation that will prevent you from jeopardising your health or feeling that you have to leave your job.

Step two: Understand your boss

When you come to look more closely at your relationship with your boss, the first thing to do is to realise how much of it is due to the structure of the organisation—for example, your boss necessarily has to give you tasks, some of which you may not enjoy—and how much is due to truly unreasonable behaviour.

Looking at the wider issues in the organisation may provide the key to the problem. 'Difficult boss syndrome' is rarely caused simply by a personality clash: more often than not, there are broader organisational factors that can go some way to explaining seemingly unreasonable behaviour.

✔ However uncomfortable it may feel, try putting yourself in your boss's shoes. Recognise the objectives that define his or her role and think through the pressures they are under.

✔ Make a mental list of your boss's strengths, preferred working style, idiosyncrasies, values, and beliefs. Observe his or her behaviour and reactions, and watch where he or she chooses to focus attention.

This will help you deepen your understanding. Very often, when we feel disliked or when we dislike someone, we avoid building this understanding and instead look for ways of avoiding the issues.

TOP TIP

If your boss is making work intolerable because of his or her moody and bad-tempered behaviour, try to work out how you could influence the situation for the better. Observe his or her behaviour to see if there is a pattern in it, and then try to broach this issue, letting your boss know how his or her mood swings affect you. Use assertive language and ask if there is anything you can do to alleviate the cause of the problem. If the behaviour persists, consult your human resources department to see if there are any formal procedures in place to deal with such a situation.

Step three: Compare the way you both perceive your role

As part of the process of understanding your boss, compare the perceptions you both have of your role and the criteria used to judge your success. You may feel that you're performing well, but if you're putting your energy into tasks that your boss does not feel are relevant, you will be seen as performing poorly.

Take the initiative to explore your boss's expectations and agree on your objectives. This will clarify your role and give you a better idea of how to progress in the organisation.

TOP TIP

Lack of communication often contributes to workplace misunderstandings. If you feel like you're missing out on opportunities or being denied information because you're not one of your boss's favourites, try approaching him or her with information about what you're doing and talk about your methods and goals. If your boss persists in denying you the information you need, you may have a case of bullying against him or her.

Step four: Understand yourself

Having scrutinised your boss and developed a greater understanding of him or her, you should try doing the same kind of exercise on yourself. Sometimes a lack of self-knowledge leads to us being surprised by our reactions and the feedback we get. It's a good idea to ask for input from your friends and colleagues while you're doing this as it's hard to judge how you come across to others.

- ✔ Ask your colleagues what they observe when you interact with your boss, how you come across to them, and how you could manage your communication differently. Although their perceptions may not represent the absolute truth about you, they nonetheless reflect the image you create.

- ✔ Think through some of the past encounters you've had with your boss and consider them objectively, perhaps with a friend or colleague who knows you well. Maybe this situation happens over and over again, which suggests that you harbour a value or belief that is being repeatedly compromised. If you can understand what this is, you can learn to manage these tricky situations more effectively.

- ✔ Consider changing your behaviour. This often prompts a reciprocal behavioural change in your boss. If you don't change anything about the way you interact with your boss, the relationship will remain unaltered, so this is definitely worth a try.

For example, perhaps you value attention to detail, but your boss is a big-picture person. Every time you ask for more detailed information, you'll be drawing attention to one of your boss's vulnerabilities, and he or she is likely to become unco-operative or irritated by your request.

Once you've observed your respective patterns, you can begin to work around them or accommodate them more calmly and objectively.

Step five: Remember that the relationship is mutual

In order to be effective, managers need a co-operative and productive team. But in order to be part of such a team, each member needs their manager to provide the resources and support they need to do their job properly. An unsupportive boss can be just as nightmarish as a vindictive one.

When managers neglect to give their employees the information and feedback they need, employees are forced to second-guess their boss's requirements. This inevitably leads to misunderstandings on both sides. The knock-on effects of this are an atmosphere of distrust and ill will, and mutual recriminations—not to mention the negative impact on the organisation's productivity levels.

✔ Ask for the information and resources you require, or find other ways to get these, as this will put you in control of the situation and protect you from the need to improvise.

Nightmare situations can arise when employees' needs aren't met. Some people become angry and resentful of the manager's authority; some find ways of challenging decisions in order to assert their own power; and others develop agendas of their own that are neither helpful nor productive.

Relationships where the balance of power is weighted very heavily in one person's favour are a recipe for revolution! It is rare in business to find relationships where there is absolutely *no* reciprocal power. Nevertheless, it's important to remember that if you're no longer willing to spend time managing your difficult boss, you still have the ultimate power: you can just walk away.

TOP TIP

If your boss is making you feel miserable by constantly making negative and derisive comments about the way you work, you need to find a private moment when you can explain how this makes you feel and ask your boss to stop doing it. You could suggest that he or she gives you clear guidelines and constructive feedback that will help you to meet his or her expectations and develop your talents. Point out that constant nagging affects the way you work and that you would be much more effective if he or she took a positive interest in what you do. If the negativity continues, you may decide to lodge a complaint of discrimination against your boss. If you take this route, make sure you have a record of the incidents and a note of any witnesses present. It's also a good idea to seek further advice from your human resources department if your company has one.

Common mistakes

✗ You take your boss's behaviour personally

It is very tempting to take the behaviour of a difficult boss personally. However, it is very unlikely that *you* are the problem. It may be something you do, it may be the values you hold, or it may be that you remind your boss of someone he or she doesn't get on with. The only person who loses out if you take it personally is you.

✗ You don't remain detached

Many difficult relationships deteriorate to the point where they are fraught with contempt and confrontation. This is never helpful in a work setting and only makes matters uncomfortable for everyone. If you find yourself being drawn into an angry exchange, try to remain emotionally detached and listen actively to what is being said to (or shouted at) you. It may provide you with clues about why the situation has developed and allow you to get straight to the point of concern. Ask for a private review afterwards to explore the incident. You may find that this brings to the surface issues that are relatively easy to deal with and that will prevent further outbursts from occurring.

✗ You never confront the issue

Because facing up to difficult people is not an easy thing to do, many people avoid biting the bullet. However, this will only prolong a miserable situation. Acquiescence enables bullying to thrive and allows the aggressors to hold power. Break the cycle by taking responsibility for your share of the problem and examining what it is you're doing to provoke conflict between you and your boss. Doing nothing is not a viable option.

STEPS TO SUCCESS

- ✔ Don't neglect the problem—for the sake of your health, if nothing else.
- ✔ Try to see both sides of the issue.
- ✔ Ask for impartial help from colleagues if you feel too emotionally involved.
- ✔ Identify and resolve areas of ambiguity in order to reduce the possibility of misunderstandings and dissatisfaction.
- ✔ Don't take it personally . . .
- ✔ . . . but remember that you might need to change too.

Useful links

Bully Online:
www.bullyonline.org
ImproveNow.com:
www.improvenow.com

Monster.com:

http://midcareer.monster.com/articles/careerdevelopment/stresseffects

TroubleAtWork:

www.troubleatwork.org.uk

4 Using non-verbal communication

It's widely recognised that the majority of information about human behaviour is conveyed through non-verbal signals. Being able to understand and use this powerful but subtle form of communication will help you shape the kinds of relationship you have with people, and this in turn will enable you to steer your way through difficult, political situations and deal with difficult, political people.

Non-verbal communication involves many different 'channels' that convey meaning beyond what is being said. These include gestures, body movements, facial expressions, and even vocal tone and pitch. Much of the non-verbal information we get from people comes from the eyes. This explains why it's often hard to convey subtle meanings over the telephone or through the written word. It's not an exact science, although we sometimes make judgments as if it were.

Since non-verbal behaviour, or body language, is such a natural part of our communication toolkit, its interpretation offers a key to greater human understanding and relationship building. However, this art should be treated with a degree of caution. Misinterpretation, especially when

dealing in a highly political organisation, can have damaging consequences.

Researchers into non-verbal behaviour agree that between 55 and 65% of all communication is done non-verbally. It's also generally accepted that the verbal part of communication is used to convey information, while the non-verbal part is used to convey values, feelings, and attitudes—the things that build rapport.

Understanding non-verbal behaviour: Gestures

The six most universal human emotions—happiness, anger, sadness, envy, fear, and love—can be seen on the face of anyone in the world, for example, in the form of smiles and scowls. Some widely-used (although not universal) gestures include the 'I don't know' shrug, a 'yes' nod, and a side-to-side head shake, meaning 'no'. Gestures that convey different messages in different cultures include the thumbs up and the 'V' sign. Although well-established in United Kingdom as signs for OK and victory respectively, they have offensive alternative meanings in other cultures!

Many gestures come in 'clusters'. If you look at people during a meeting, you are likely to see gestures involving hands (they may be signalling that they are evaluating what is being said by balancing their chin on their thumb with their middle finger running along their bottom lip and their index finger pointing up their cheek), their limbs (one arm may be clamped against the body by the other elbow), and their entire bodies (if someone's torso is leaning back from the vertical, that person is signalling distance from what is being said). This cluster of non-verbal gestures indicates that the listener is reserving judgment on what is being said. If you feel that a cluster of gestures is conveying something about what the person really thinks, ask them to share their thoughts.

Step one: Match and mirror

If you watch two people talking in a relaxed and unselfconscious manner, you may notice that their bodies have taken on a similar demeanour. Both may have crossed their legs, or settled into their chairs in similar postures. If they are eating or drinking, they may do so at the same rate. This is called *matching* or *mirroring*, and it occurs naturally between two people who feel that they're on the same wavelength.

✔ Matching and mirroring can be used consciously as a technique to achieve rapport with someone, but you need to be subtle. Exaggerated mirroring looks like mimicry, and the other person is likely to feel embarrassed or angry.

✔ Observe what your counterparts do with their bodies. Then follow the pattern of their non-verbal communication and reflect it back. When this feels natural, see if you can take the lead by changing your body position and watch to see if they follow. Very often they do. Once you begin to get a feel for this process, see if you can use it in a situation that is problematic.

TOP TIP

Sometimes, you might inadvertently convey the wrong message—perhaps you have a habit of using an expression or gesture that is commonly accepted to mean one thing when you really mean something different. A nervous laugh, for example, might indicate that you think you're being funny. You may, in fact, be trying to communicate something serious, but are nervous because it's a delicate subject. Training can help correct the most obvious quirks in your non-verbal lexicon. In the meantime it might help to acknowledge your idiosyncrasies publicly so people don't get the wrong impression.

Understanding non-verbal behaviour: Facial expressions

Most non-verbal signals conveyed by the face are done so by the eyes. Good eye contact is an effective way of building rapport. Not only can you 'read' the other's disposition, you can also convey, very subtly, messages that will reinforce what you are saying.

However, too much eye contact can be intrusive or too intimate. Those who do not want to be exposed on the 'soul level' may use techniques to break or block eye contact. This includes eye movements such as the 'over the shoulder stare', or the long, fluttery, blink that effectively draws the shutters down. In a business setting, it's important to confine your gaze to the eyes and forehead, and forego the more intimate glance to the lips or upper body. If you hold your stare for too long, it may be considered hostile, so try to limit the time to around two thirds of the conversation. If you reduce the timing to below one third, you may appear timid or 'shifty'.

Step two: Speak the same language

While the language we use is clearly not one of the components of non-verbal behaviour, it's an important part of that same unconscious and instinctive toolkit we use to communicate with others. According to neurolinguistic programming (NLP)—the science of tapping into the unconscious mind to reveal what is going on beneath the surface—language can indicate a great deal about how an individual views the world. Depending on which of the five senses they subconsciously favour, people may fall into one of five noticeable types:

- visual (sight)
- auditory (hearing)

- kinaesthetic (touch)
- olfactory (smell)
- gustatory (taste)

You can establish rapport with people more effectively by paying attention to their individual preferences for 'sensual' cues.

✔ When talking to someone you don't know well, listen to the kinds of words he or she selects. Once you have identified which of the five categories (explained above) they belong to, you can respond by using the same kind of language.

In other words, when you are building rapport with someone, using the same kind of language significantly enhances the level of understanding between you.

Different types of vocabulary

Here are some examples of the vocabulary the five different types of people use:

- **visual language** includes terms like *appear*, *show*, *focused*, *well-defined*, *in light of*, *dim view*, *get a perspective on*. For example, a person might say something like, 'I have a *vision* of what this organisation will *look* like in five year's time. I can *see* that it will take lots of energy to create what is in my *mind's eye*'. You can respond similarly: 'You build a very *clear picture* for me. I can *see* that this will be a challenge, but your *farsightedness* will surely enable you to reach your *dream*'.

- **auditory language** includes terms like *listen*, *tune in/out*, *rumour*, *clear as a bell*, *unheard of*, *word for word*, and *be all ears*. An auditory person might say, 'I *hear* that you have been promoted. You must have done a *resoundingly* good job!' You could respond, 'Yes, I have been *called* upon to *sound* out the market and *ring* some changes in the way we sell our products'.
- **kinaesthetic language** includes terms like *sense*, *feel*, *move towards*, *grasp*, *get hold of*, *solid*, *make contact*, *touch*, *concrete*, *pull some strings*, and *sensitive*.
- **olfactory language** includes terms like *smell*, *odour*, *rotten*, *aromatic*, and *fragrance*.
- **gustatory language** includes terms like *bitter*, *sweet*, *sour*, *salty*, and other taste-related words.

Step three: Listen actively

Active listening is a rare skill, but it's very effective in helping you build rapport with people and avoid the kind of misunderstandings that land you in awkward political situations. It can also yield valuable information, enabling us to do our jobs more efficiently.

✔ Demonstrate that you have understood and are interested in what is being said in conversation. This kind of active listening requires good eye contact, lots of head nods, and responses such as 'Ah ha', 'Mmmm', and 'I understand what you mean'.

✔ Summarise what has been said to demonstrate your understanding. Ask open questions such as, 'Can you tell me more about . . . ?' and 'What do you think . . . ?'. These questions encourage further communication and enrich what is being communicated.

TOP TIP

People often try to cover up anger at work. However, their tone of voice, subtle changes in facial expression, and aggressive gestures are likely to convey their real emotions. For example, maybe someone will start pacing up and down or banging the table while still smiling pleasantly in an attempt to hide their true but socially unacceptable feelings. Active listening and open questions can help to defuse anger before it boils over.

Understanding non-verbal behaviour: Props

People use props to reinforce their messages, especially extensions of the hand such as pens, pointers, or even a cigarette. A prop extends the space used by the body, and makes the person appear more confident and powerful.

Adjusting a tie, fussing with the hair, or tugging at a cuff is representative of 'preening'. People often use these behaviours to endear themselves to others, although these gestures can instead be perceived as nervousness. Clenching coffee cups or wine glasses close to the body allows them to be used as defence mechanisms. They effectively close off the more vulnerable parts of the body.

The way people in a group sit can convey powerful messages about the pecking order. Taking the chair at the head of the table automatically puts someone in the controlling position. Leaning back with arms behind the head and one leg crossed horizontally across the other conveys feelings of superiority. A closed or crunched body position can mean disapproval, defensiveness, or a lack of interest.

Step four: Interpret in context

Much has been written about non-verbal communication, especially about how to read body language. This may give you insight into what is going on, but always remember to place your interpretation in context. For example, someone sitting in a meeting with his or her arms crossed is possibly being aggressive, reluctant, or disapproving. But, perhaps the person is shy, cold, or ill.

✔ Be cautious of jumping to conclusions about how someone is feeling without further information.

If you move to a new environment with a different political mentality, there could be a risk of misunderstandings at a non-verbal level. Perhaps your new boss is more emotional than your previous manager and expects a more energetic display of your enthusiasm for the job.

✔ Make sure you take time to observe what is going on around you and note how the different context makes you feel. Perhaps ask advice from someone in the new culture who shares something of your own experience—they may be able to provide a useful communications bridge.

Understanding non-verbal behaviour: Congruence

In order for non-verbal behaviour to work for you, all the non-verbal channels of communication must reinforce the message you're trying to convey. If you notice side-to-side head-shaking while someone is saying, 'I agree wholeheartedly with this decision', you may be seeing an example of incongruence; the person's words and body language are contradictory. People come across as inauthentic when one or more of their channels of communication are 'saying' opposite things.

TOP TIP

Non-verbal messages can help you spot when someone is lying. Usually, when people are communicating in a straightforward way,

their non-verbal signals are consistent with their words: they might say, 'I'm unhappy about that', and their face and body will droop too. When people are bluffing, their gestures are usually inconsistent with their speech. Someone may say, 'The deal is almost in the bag!'—but you notice a nervous body pattern, like the shifting of feet or the tapping of fingers. Unusual avoidance of eye contact or a lot of blinking can also indicate an inconsistency, which communication experts call *leakage.* Other gestures associated with lying include hiding the mouth with a hand, touching one's nose, or running a finger along the inside of a collar.

Understanding non-verbal behaviour: Territory

People travel through the world with a conceptual egg-shaped zone of personal space around their bodies, and feel invaded if others trespass into it. They often protect their territory by placing a desk between them and others, standing behind a chair or counter, or shielding themselves with a handbag or briefcase.

It is interesting to watch people in groups. If you see two or three men talking, you might notice them shifting their weight from one foot to the other. This is part of a ritual of creating territorial boundaries. They might also make themselves appear taller by rocking forward onto the balls of their feet to indicate power and confidence. When women are grouped, they are much more likely to mirror each other's non-verbal behaviour in an attempt to build lateral bridges.

It is, therefore, essential to place any 'bodywatching' observations *in context*, as most non-verbal communication is part of a broader dialogue.

Common mistakes

✗ You lack subtlety

People new to the techniques of non-verbal communication can be over-enthusiastic practitioners. Observe yourself objectively to make sure you aren't offending others by broadly mimicking their speech or behaviour. Remember that most people instinctively send and interpret non-verbal signals all the time: don't assume you're the only one who's aware of non-verbal undercurrents. Finally, stay true to yourself. Be aware of your own natural style, and don't adopt behaviour that is incompatible with it.

✗ You over-interpret

When people become aware of the power of body language, they can go overboard and think they have revealed a whole world of silent messages. However, false interpretations can cause damaging misunderstandings. Remember to take account of the context and do not jump to conclusions.

✗ You try to bluff

Thinking you can bluff by deliberately altering your body language can do more harm than good. Unless you are a practised actor, it will be hard to overcome the body's inability to lie. There will always be mixed messages, signs that your channels of communication are not congruent. This is called *leakage* and it will be seen in one way or another.

✗ You ignore context

Putting too much store by someone's non-verbal signals can lead to misinterpretation and misunderstandings. It's important to understand the context in which the signals are being transmitted and think through the possible scenarios before jumping in.

✗ You rush in with an accusation based on someone's body language

Accusing someone of something that they are not guilty of, based on erroneous observations, can be embarrassing and damaging. Always verify your interpretation through another channel before rushing in. You could say something like, 'I get the feeling you are uncomfortable with this course of action. Would you like to add something to the discussion?' This will draw out the real message and force the individual to come clean, or withdraw his or her bodily objections.

STEPS TO SUCCESS

- ✔ Watch the body language of others and mirror it.
- ✔ Observe the language used by those you wish to influence, listening out for 'sensual' cues.
- ✔ Listen actively, letting the other person know you are interested.
- ✔ Think carefully before interpreting non-verbal signals—there could be many reasons for unusual behaviour.
- ✔ Look out for leakage. It can help you identify when someone is hiding something.
- ✔ Remember that other people know about these techniques and will be able to spot any obvious attempts to influence their opinions. Be subtle!

Useful links

NLP training and resources:
www.altfeld.com/mastery/seminars/desc-sb1.html
PPI Business NLP:
www.ppimk.com
Rider University Clinical Psychology Department
www.rider.edu/users/suler/bodylang.html

5 Managing others' perceptions

We all hold differing views of the world, partly because of our different cultural backgrounds, life experiences, and personal values. Naturally, these influence the way we interact with one another—they are part of what makes human societies and organisations political. Our behaviour, competences, style, and approach further affect our relationships.

However, we aren't entirely products of our past—we're consciously capable of modifying our conduct and, in turn, affecting the impression we make on others. Learning how to project a positive image of ourselves can be an invaluable tool in many areas of our lives, but especially in the workplace. In senior management roles, it's particularly important to understand and manage the way we're regarded.

This isn't as difficult as you might think. Although it requires a good deal of thought, motivation, and self-awareness, with practice you'll soon find it easier to communicate effectively with difficult people, motivate staff, and lead them in the desired direction.

Step one: Overcome your misgivings

1 It's not about deception

Some people feel that changing the way you're perceived is a form of deception; they believe it involves pretending you're something you're not. However, managing perceptions is more about shedding light on your positive aspects while minimising the visibility of your weaknesses. It's not about deceit. It's about letting your true talents shine through.

2 It's a part of life

We live in a culture where people and organisations spend enormous sums of money hiring others to manage perceptions. The same skills used by advertising and public relations companies can be employed by you to influence those around you.

✔ Be aware of the impression your behaviour creates. This is the first step towards perception management. Gradually, you can develop skills that help you to manage your behaviour in a way that will move your career forward in the direction you want.

3 It can help you in your career

In the modern employment market, there's a greater onus on autonomy. Careers are no longer managed by organisations, but are directed by individuals themselves. You're judged not only on what you do, but on how you do it—so evaluation by others now plays an important role in your career. People who can manage perceptions are likely to receive more offers and find fewer obstacles in their career path.

TOP TIP

Take care of your relationships as you move up the career ladder, because you may encounter the same people later when you're moving back down! People can harbour grudges for years, and you don't want to risk encountering an unforgiving individual in a position of influence. If you find it impossible to change your attitude, you'd better have skills that make you indispensable!

Step two: Understand how you're perceived

To understand how others view you, you must have an accurate understanding of yourself. Building self-awareness requires courage, commitment, and forgiveness.

✔ Firstly, encourage informal feedback from trusted peers and managers. Remember that people will be giving you *their* opinions and these may not resonate with yours—

you may be surprised at the way you're perceived. Try to remain objective and find out where these views have come from.

✔ Use more formal tools that enable you to understand yourself, such as psychometric tests and personality profiles. The feedback from these is sometimes easier to manage because it's objective and has no third-party involvement.

✔ Sometimes, 360-degree surveys are used to gather the views of different audiences, both inside and outside the business. These tend to focus on behaviour and competence. Be aware of the differences between the two. While both may be learned and modified, changing behaviour usually involves altering personality traits and perceptions and may be more difficult than acquiring new skills.

✔ When reviewing test results, try not to concentrate solely on personal information that is hurtful. Look for patterns in the feedback, and reflect on when and why these may have arisen. Pressure can often allow unintentional behaviour to come to the surface and this may have given rise to impressions that you would like to change.

TOP TIP

People generally hold onto first impressions, and it's difficult to replace them with something more to your liking. Changing

how others view you requires a consistent flow of new messages, and this means persistent awareness and self-evaluation—both of which take time and energy to develop.

Step three: Determine your strategy

Before embarking on any perception management strategy, establish what your goals are, how you're going to reach them, and how you'll track your success.

✔ Don't be too ambitious at first: focus on one thing you can change that will create an immediate impression.

✔ Think of the context in which you're working, and use your feedback to select your initial goals.

Do

- Increase your own awareness.
- Be aware of your impact on others and interpret the signals they transmit to you.
- Be aware of the effect of pressure on you and how this looks to others.
- Be visible at strategic moments.
- Gently encourage feedback from people whose opinions you value.
- Allow others to have their choices.
- Give yourself time to change.

- Be consistent, patient, and forgiving of yourself and others.

Don't

- React emotionally to the feedback you receive.
- Get defensive.
- Become de-motivated.
- Become sycophantic.
- Get too big for your boots and try too hard too quickly.
- Expect too much.
- Embroil others in your views of yourself.
- Pester people for feedback.
- Be political or manipulative in your behaviour.

In a nutshell, perception management is all about creating an impression through conscious activities and awareness of your audience and the impact you have upon them. To succeed, you must:

✔ define your target audience

✔ be conscious of their values

✔ adjust your communication style

✔ encourage feedback

✔ be aware of how you adjust and adapt your behaviour

Step four: Gather support

While there may be encouragement to change your behaviour initially, remember that there may also be reactions to those changes. People are accustomed to the 'old' you and may have difficulty adjusting to the 'new' you. It's therefore important to do four things:

- ✔ Communicate your intentions to people who may be affected. If you have a formal annual performance appraisal, make it a 'learning objective', as this is likely to win more support and forgiveness if things don't work out quite the way you wish. You'll also receive more praise when you're successful.

- ✔ Gain support from your manager or key members of your team to help keep you focused. A good support group is essential when seeking to change something about yourself. Extraordinary transformations have been achieved with the help of groups such as Alcoholics Anonymous and Weight Watchers.

- ✔ Find a coach to provide ongoing guidance. A coach will be able to offer impartial observations and encourage you to continue, or change, your strategy as you move forward. Coaching takes time and commitment, so you'll need to allow for this in your work plan.

- ✔ Evaluate your progress at each milestone in your plan, either formally or informally. It's important to gather informal feedback regularly, but make sure you give people enough time to observe your new behaviour before asking for their opinions. You might warn those whom you're going to approach for feedback, so they can consciously pay attention to your behaviour. A more formal option is to revisit the 360-degree questionnaire and see whether others have noticed the change.

Don't lose heart if the changes in your approach aren't immediately recognised by others. It may take some months for the changes to be noticed, so consistency and perseverance are essential. In the meantime, keeping a journal to record your progress is a good way of boosting your motivation.

TOP TIP

If you wish to change someone's impression of you, you must first understand both that person's existing perception and the one you wish to create. You then need to create a bridge between the two. Observe the person's values and behaviour and find an opportunity to convey a different message. However, you must be honest in the way you portray yourself. If you create an impression that isn't essentially *you,* the deception will be easy to spot, simply because living a lie is extraordinarily difficult to sustain.

Common mistakes

✗ You become impatient

It's easy to be impatient for results and give up too quickly. Behavioural change isn't as easy as learning a new skill; it requires dedication, commitment, and consistency. It's only through constant repetition and reinforcement of your new behaviour that people's perceptions will change.

✗ You don't ask for feedback

Some people are embarrassed to ask for feedback and help, particularly when they're in senior roles. This is because many forms of behaviour are habitual, and some may even have contributed to previous promotions. However, conduct appropriate to some roles may not be right for others. Promotion to a management position can highlight these differences, when relationships suddenly become much more important than technical skills. In this situation, use a new project or a particular aspect of your new role as a test-bed for the new you.

✗ You aim too high

In trying to change behaviour, people can be too ambitious and therefore lose the support of others. While it's important to be enthusiastic, try to understate rather than overstate your goals. It's always easier to deal with the surprise of your audience, rather than their disappointment.

STEPS TO SUCCESS

- ✔ Acknowledge the importance of perception management.
- ✔ Find out how people perceive you and how that differs from your own perception.
- ✔ Start small: begin by changing only one aspect of your image.
- ✔ Define your target audience, align your values with theirs, and adjust your communication style accordingly.
- ✔ Encourage feedback and involve other people in helping you sustain the change.
- ✔ Don't expect too much too soon.

Useful links

Alinea Group:
www.alineagroup.com/ Impression%20Management.htm
All About Human Resources:
http://humanresources.about.com
Global Image Group:
www.globalimagegrp.com

6 Networking for success

Networks are built on direct and indirect contacts in the personal, professional, or organisational arenas. The overriding goal of networking is to build and manage productive relationships, and this is particularly useful for anyone affected by office politics. For example, if you need advice on how to deal with a fraught relationship at work, sharing the problem with others or calling on contacts in your network can help you find the help you need to deal with that situation. If you feel that you need to move on, your network may be able to help you find a new job.

Whatever your needs, it's important to respect and nurture your networks, as if you neglect or exploit them, they'll collapse and you'll be left without resources—and probably when you need them most.

You have networks already, without realising it, such as family, friends, and your school or university contacts. You may also be part of a professional body or have some expertise that links you to others whom you may not have met yet.

Step one: Map out your networks

Taking a conscious approach to networking can be hard at the beginning. Remember, though, that the 'movers and shakers' in your office—those that play the politics game well (so well, in fact, that you don't realise they're doing it)—had to start somewhere.

The first thing to do is to map out the network that you already have; many people are surprised to see just how extensive their network is when they go through this exercise and how much untapped potential is there.

These networks can be sub-divided as follows:

- personal—friends, family
- organisational—teams, project groups, committees
- professional—associates, colleagues, clients, suppliers
- strategic—inter-organisational, political

✔ Put your name in the middle of a large piece of paper surrounded by the names of your present contacts and draw the links out. Connect the names with lines to show the relationships between them. You could use different colours for different networks and/or different widths of lines for the depth of relationship.

✔ When you get in touch with people already in your network, ask them to suggest other people who share your areas of interest. Add their names to the map and extend it as if it were a spreading family tree.

TOP TIP

You might feel uncomfortable about networking because you think it's all about playing political games to meet personal goals. Certainly it can feel like this for those who are being used by someone who doesn't understand the importance of relationships. The best approach is *do-as-you-would-be-done-by*: you put yourself in the other person's shoes and ask yourself whether your demands are reasonable and whether you can do anything for them in return.

Step two: Identify your style

See if you can identify your natural networking style from the three types described below.

- **Conscious networkers** have clear goals; they recognise the gaps in their network and identify opportunities to build relationships for the future.
- **Intuitive networkers** often feel happiest mixing with people so they can follow their instincts and interests. These networks are built on serendipity and the networker may be unaware of the value they have.
- **Political networkers** build relationships to fuel their ambitions and to win power. Their relationships often don't 'make sense' to observers, but there is bound to be a reason behind them.

TOP TIP

There are many ways of building and nurturing networks. Not all require you to be an extrovert or display high levels of confidence. If, for example, you're uncomfortable in a room full of people you don't know, think about what you could offer others that doesn't demand a high level of social interaction. You could contact others on the phone, by e-mail, or the Web to build your network. These relationships can be just as valuable as more personal ones.

Step three: Clarify your goals and plan your path

To be a successful networker you need to have an ideal result in mind. This will focus your energies and help you to convey exactly what you need so that others can assist you. It also helps you make good decisions, as each will be made in the context of your overall goal.

Four primary goals

These are the main objectives that should motivate your networking activity:

- **Information.** In order to find the latest information you need to identify your sources, sometimes called *hubs* or *informers*. These people are the repositories of useful information. They often understand market trends and developments and are able to point you towards opportunities or provide new approaches and perspectives on a situation. However, information can sometimes be tainted by gossip or a political agenda, so make sure that you consult with a variety of sources to get a balanced picture.
- **Development.** Continuous development is important for anyone who wants to get on in his or her career. Use your network to seek guidance and feedback, and allow it to act as a mouthpiece that informs others of your achievements or your willingness to take on new challenges. Your network can also alert you to valuable development and career opportunities.
- **Support.** Ask yourself: Who should I surround myself with? Who are the people that give me consistent support? Who acts as a sounding board when I need to put my thoughts in order? And who will help me achieve my objectives by combining their efforts with mine? Don't take these people for granted. Think about how you can reward them for the value they bring to you.
- **Influence.** Some people in your network may be able to influence your future. They'll be prepared to give you resources, to promote your cause, and increase your visibility among the 'right' people. You

might find it helpful to have a mentor with whom you could discuss your decisions, from whom you could learn new things, and who will act as an influencer on your behalf.

Step four: Develop networking behaviour

There is an unwritten code of ethics for good networking practices. If you look after networks with care and attention, you'll reap the rewards.

✔ Be open-minded.

✔ Keep commitments.

✔ Do as you would be done by.

✔ Don't be afraid to ask.

✔ Give generously.

✔ Recognise problems and deal with them directly.

✔ Always say 'thank you'.

Keep your eyes and ears open for chances to help others. By involving yourself in the lives of the people who belong to your network you'll soon learn of the sorts of things they like and value. An article on a topic of interest to them, information on an event that they would enjoy, a ticket to a concert or community event, anything of this sort will reinforce the relationships that you value in your network.

TOP TIP

One way to avoid making people feel exploited when you ask them for a favour, is to offer them something of value. You may have noticed that they have a particular interest or a need for some information. If you anticipate and offer some information or a contact tailored to that person, you'll be able to pave the way for a reciprocal favour. Be sure to build in plenty of goodwill, though, so that you don't gain a reputation for being someone who makes offers simply to get something in return.

Understanding and investing time and energy in your networks benefits both the professional and personal areas of your life. By constantly monitoring and managing your networks you can keep a good balance.

✔ Be visible. If you know how to network and how to identify the hubs and informers, people will get to know you. This will help you to network more effectively.

✔ Boost your employability. Successful people know that the way to good opportunities can come from a network. So a network that includes people in your organisation can actually reinforce your impact at work and the impression you make on your employer.

TOP TIP

Don't be put off getting in contact with people because they're difficult to get hold of. It's surprising how few people you need to go through in order to reach someone you wish to meet, however remote they are. Think about the links in your network and the contexts in which people live or work. Do any of these overlap with those of the person you wish to contact? In most cases it takes a maximum of four contacts to reach almost anyone!

Common mistakes

✗ **You don't show appreciation for others' help**

Many people forget to show appreciation once their networking goal has been achieved. People like to know when their assistance has been successful and welcome a brief thank you note or other sign of appreciation. If you repeatedly fail to thank people if they've helped you, they will, quite reasonably, be reluctant to assist you again. Avoid being selfish and always say thank you for support you've received.

✗ **You can't say 'no'**

Seeking to build relationships non-stop—just in case—can quickly tire you out. Learn to say 'no' and control the amount of time and energy you put into networking.

STEPS TO SUCCESS

- ✔ Map out your current network of contacts like a family tree, and look for ways you can branch out.
- ✔ Establish your goals and plan your route.
- ✔ Identify where the obstacles lie and think of ways to deal with them.
- ✔ Look after your network. Treat your contacts as you hope they would treat you.
- ✔ Always say thank you for advice or support that you receive from your network.

Useful links

Friends Reunited:
www.friendsreunited.co.uk
I-resign.com:
www.i-resign.com/uk/workinglife/viewarticle_125.asp
Management-resources.org:
www.management-resources.org

Dealing with office romances

As we spend so much time at work, it's no surprise that many people have romantic relationships with colleagues. In fact, according to a survey quoted in the *Guardian* newspaper in January 2004, more than 60% of people have had a relationship of this type at work, and more than half said it had affected their work.

Many people who had an office romance have regretted it, for one reason or another. A lot of office politics is based on jealousy, with people feeling 'slighted' for either real or imaginary reasons, so if you work in an environment where office politics is rife, office romances (or the gossip surrounding them) can get out of hand. This chapter offers advice for anyone in an office romance or anyone who is the manager of someone involved in one.

Step one: Think about the pros and cons

People find romance in the office for many reasons. Most people working full-time spend over 35 hours a week at work, so they necessarily build friendships with others there.

Conversations can spring up in the canteen or by the photocopier or kettle. If you work in a very specialised industry, work might be the one place where you can find people who share some of your interests.

✔ It's easy to get carried away in the first flush of attraction for someone, but if you work with that person too, think about the following:

- does the company you work for actively rule out dating at work?
- is the other person your boss, or are you theirs?
- how would you deal with office gossip if you became a couple?
- will there be accusations of favouritism?
- will you still be able to do your job properly?
- how would you cope if the relationship ended badly?

I Dating a peer

Going out with someone who has the same level of responsibilities as you, if not exactly the same job, might look like the safest option. If nothing else, spending so much time at work with someone else means that you have a good chance of getting to know them quite well before you become a couple. On the downside, working with your partner means that you never really get a break from them. You might find that you end up talking about work a lot even when you're not there, and if you have to work together on a project that becomes fraught, friction could be introduced into the relationship.

TOP TIP

Remember that if you work near to where your partner does (on the same floor or at a neighbouring desk, for example), you may find it hard if other people try to flirt with him or her. This will not only make you unhappy, but will also cause your work to suffer.

If your partner does have the same job as you, things could get tricky if the chance of a promotion comes up. Only one person can get that new post, and if you've both applied but one of you is the successful applicant, things are likely to be tense for at least a little while.

Remember that in extreme cases, people who were once in a relationship find it impossible to work with each other once it's over. Some people even go to the lengths of changing their core working hours so that they can avoid their ex-partner. Others may decide to leave the company completely.

2 Dating a junior member of staff

If you are your partner's manager, things are much more complicated. Even if you break the news to other people before they find out for themselves, some people are much more likely to think that your partner will be getting preferential treatment in terms of responsibilities, pay, and promotion prospects, for example.

Even if you make a concerted effort not to treat your partner differently from anyone else, you may find that you do it subconsciously in one of two ways: either you'll be easier on your partner than you are with other team members, or you'll try to counteract accusations of favouritism by being harder on your partner than you need to be.

You also need to think about how you'd deal with situations that may crop up in a downturn. You may have to make your partner redundant, for example. Would your relationship be able to survive that?

As with any office romance, if things don't go as well as you'd expected and you break up, the aftermath can be difficult. The atmosphere may be terrible, he or she may refuse to work with you, and may want to be transferred to another team.

3 Dating your boss or a senior member of staff

Again, whispers of favouritism may start to build dramatically if you start a relationship with your boss or someone much higher up the career ladder than you. If your partner is your manager, you're putting yourself in a potentially difficult situation whether things go well or badly. If you get a promotion, some people are bound to think (and to say out loud) that you didn't win it on your own merits, but just because of your relationship. If your relationship ends and your career takes a nose-dive at the same time, you may feel that events in your private life are affecting your professional life and you're being treated unfairly.

4 Dating a key supplier, external partner, or competitor

Sometimes, office romances can be 'one step removed' in that the people involved don't work for the same company, but work for two companies that work very closely together. For example, one person may work for a printer and the other person for a paper supplier. While you may not see your partner all day every day at work, your relationship may still run the risk of damaging your company's interests if it were to end badly.

Step two: Find out if your company has a policy on this issue

Some businesses do see office romances as something other than innocent flirtation that makes the day go by more quickly. For example, they worry that the romances:

- encourage conflict amongst colleagues (if someone feels jealous of another person, for example)
- reduce productivity (if the couple spend a good part of their working day talking to, e-mailing, or phoning each other for non-work issues)
- compromise decision-making
- may allow competitors to gain an advantage

Businesses tend to tackle the issue of office romances in one of three ways:

- they ignore them.
- they are opposed to them. In the United States, some companies have 'no-dating' policies, which are intended to prevent problems arising from employee relationships in the workplace (such as preferential treatment or claims of sexual harassment if a relationship breaks down). The policies define what constitutes acceptable and unacceptable behaviour and what action will be taken if the terms of the policy are violated. No-dating policies are still a relatively small-scale way of dealing with romance at work, and concerns have been raised that they may adversely affect employees' right to privacy.
- they realise that they can and do happen and as a result set up some type of formal way of recording them to protect both themselves and the employees. Some businesses have adopted another practice that originated in the United States, which is asking employees to notify their managers if they enter into a relationship at work and to sign an agreement that states that the relationship is consensual. These agreements are sometimes called 'cupid' or 'love' contracts and may be used where an employer requires notification of such relationships, especially between supervisors and their subordinates. The agreement may also stipulate that the relationship will not affect or interfere with the work of those involved.

✔ If you're involved in a long-term relationship with a colleague, check what your company's views are on office romances (someone in human resources should be able to help you.) If there's a policy in place, comply fully and tell your manager as soon as you can.

Step three: If you decide to go ahead . . .

1 Be sure it's what you want

A kiss at the Christmas party is one thing, but a full-blown relationship with a colleague is a different matter. It could affect your job and your prospects radically, so be as sure as you can that it's a good idea for you. If you're new to the company, try to find out discreetly if the other party has a history of going out with people from the office or has a partner at home that he or she is keeping quiet about!

TOP TIP

If you feel you're being pressurised into a relationship you don't want, take action immediately. You have a right to go to work without being harassed. Talk to your boss about the situation if you can, but if your boss is the other party, contact someone in human resources or your boss's line manager.

2 Be discreet

✔ If you're in a relationship at work or are about to embark on one, it's important to be discreet. Don't tell anyone who doesn't need to know, and act appropriately at all times in any work dealings with your partner. If anyone does ask you directly about your relationship, be honest and say 'yes, I am dating X', but there's no need to go any further than that. People will find something and someone else to talk about soon enough.

TOP TIP

Think about how to deal with issues such as arriving or leaving the office together. If you work physically close to your partner and your colleagues are unaware of your relationship, they may quickly put two and two together if you start to turn up or go home at the same time. Think about how you want to play this so that you keep the fuss to a minimum but also cut down on the stress you may be feeling at having to keep a big part of your life secret.

3 Do your job

Remember that even though the office has given you the opportunity to find a partner, you still need to do your job when you get there.

✔ If you have to work closely with your partner, keep all your communications professional. Take special care when you're phoning or e-mailing them, and don't write personal information in e-mails as some companies will monitor them. You may also accidentally send the e-mail to the wrong person, which is bad enough if it's someone inside your company, but much worse if it's an external contact!

- ✔ Don't spend a lot of time dropping by your partner's desk unless you really need to—remember that you'll not only be disturbing any colleagues sitting close, but also giving them the opportunity to hear what you're saying. This is the type of thing that can annoy other people and make a difficult or sensitive situation much worse.

Step four: Keep calm if things go wrong

1 If your office romance has gone wrong:

- ✔ If you signed a 'love' contract, tell your manager.
- ✔ Keep your own counsel. Don't tell anyone who doesn't really need to know.
- ✔ Even if the other party has behaved badly or unfairly, don't badmouth them to other people who work with them closely. As with most office gossip, what you say will be turned into something a hundred times worse by the time it's been through the rumour mill.
- ✔ Keep a professional distance. This will be hard at first, but if you have to work with your ex-partner often, be polite and get on with your job even if it's the last thing you might feel like doing.

- ✔ If your ex-partner behaves badly or threateningly towards you in the workplace, talk to your manager straightaway. Act quickly and don't let it escalate. Make detailed notes of exactly what happened when and whether anyone else witnessed the incident. When you talk to your boss try to remain as calm and objective as you can, however upset you feel.

2 If you're the manager of someone whose office romance has gone wrong:

- ✔ Be supportive. Try not to say 'I told you so', even if you did. Accept that the relationship happened, is now over, and try to support employees who ask for your help.

- ✔ Keep some perspective. While, naturally, you have responsibilities to step in if you feel someone has gone too far in an office relationship or if you're directly asked for help, don't get dragged into the aftermath of a messy break-up.

- ✔ Don't comment on the rights and wrongs of the situation, make disparaging comments about the other party (even if, deep-down, you think they deserve it), or promise something that you might not be able to deliver. For example, if one of the parties comes to you and demands that he or she be moved to a different department or team, say that you'll investigate and get back to him or her.

3 If you were involved in the relationship and you *are* the boss:

✔ Talk to your own manager about how best to handle the fall-out. Be completely honest, even though you may feel embarrassed. It's much better that he or she be put in the picture as soon as possible, and it's particularly important to check that procedures are followed properly if you are to avoid sexual harassment claims.

Common mistakes

✗ You tell too many people

It's exciting when you start a new relationship, and if your romance is taking place at the office it could be brightening up your work day too. If you do have an office romance, however, resist the temptation to tell everyone you know what's happening. Be discreet and don't give the resident gossips or troublemakers the opportunity to make you topic of the day.

✗ You don't check your company's policy

Even if you think an office romance is harmless, your managers might not agree. You may feel awkward, but it's worth checking with your boss (if he or she is not the other party involved) or someone from human resources whether your company has a no-dating policy or if it requires you to sign a 'love' contract.

✗ **You don't do your job**

If you're bored at work and looking for a distraction, an office romance might be just what you're looking for. The problem is that we never know how long relationships will last, so make sure that you carry on doing your job to the best of your ability so that no one can question your commitment, whatever is happening in your personal life.

✗ **You badmouth your ex-partner at work**

If your office romance doesn't last, don't tell tales or spread rumours about your now ex-partner to his or her colleagues. Break-ups are often difficult, but try to keep calm and remember that anything you say in haste will either come back to haunt you or be exaggerated by someone else, making the whole situation much worse. If your ex is rude about you, talk to your manager straightaway.

STEPS TO SUCCESS

✔ Think really hard about whether an office romance is wise for you.

✔ Check your company's policy about relationships between colleagues.

✔ Be discreet.

✔ Do your job properly and don't waste time e-mailing,

phoning, or visiting your partner constantly unless you need to talk to them about work matters.

- ✔ If you feel you're being pressurised into a relationship you don't want, talk to your boss or someone in your human resources department.
- ✔ If your office romance ends, try to keep calm while you're at work and don't badmouth your ex-partner.

Useful links

Equal Opportunities Commission:
www.eoc.org.uk
Handbag.com:
www.handbag.com/careers

8 Managing office politics in meetings

Meetings are a necessary evil in everyone's working life. Handled well, they can help those involved get to the bottom of a tricky situation, agree actions, and do something positive. Handled badly, they're not only an appalling waste of time, but a forum in which festering office politics can get out of hand. Basically, you want to get in and out as soon as possible with the least amount of fuss and all relevant decisions made so that you can get on with the rest of your day.

This chapter offers advice for anyone who has to chair a meeting in a politically-fraught office atmosphere.

Step one: Decide if you really need a meeting

In some cases, meetings are not always a good use of people's time and effort. If someone suggests that a meeting be held to discuss an issue related to your project, team, or department, think hard about whether gathering the attendees in one place is really the most efficient way forward, especially if this involves a substantial amount of travelling for some people. Could you accomplish your aims by using conference calls or videoconferencing?

You might also want to use e-mail to discuss this issue. This sounding out of potential attendees before a meeting also allows you to test the water and get an early indication of people who may clash either in terms of their personality or their approach to the subject under discussion. If all else fails, though, and a face-to-face meeting seems to be the best and least unwieldy way of agreeing action on the issue at hand, prepare as much as you can in advance.

Step two: Do the initial planning

1 Think carefully about who to invite

✔ Limit the numbers by only inviting those who really need to be there. The most productive meetings are usually those with the smallest number of people attending. If the agenda is lengthy and covers a variety of issues, consider asking people to drop in and out when their relevant section comes up.

2 Give the attendees all the relevant information in good time

✔ To make sure that all the attendees have a chance to raise their concerns during the meeting, give them plenty of notice of the meeting's time and venue and circulate a draft agenda outlining the topics to be discussed and the time limits assigned to each topic.

TOP TIP

All attendees need to be clear about the purpose of the meeting and why they have been called together. The agenda should set out what needs to be accomplished between the start and finish of the meeting.

✔ Be completely upfront about who you are inviting if you know already that the meeting may involve people who don't get on or who may have a hidden agenda. You can then prepare yourself for what may be, at times, a bumpy ride. You'll also be giving the opposing parties plenty of notice about each other's attendance. What may be a tense atmosphere will only be made worse by people being taken aback by (what will seem to them) the surprise appearance of someone they don't like.

TOP TIP

Research shows that the best time to hold a meeting is just before lunch or towards the end of the day. This motivates attendees to focus on the agenda and keep on schedule! If you're offering lunch and you're worried that a seating plan may exacerbate tensions between attendees (for example, if someone refuses to sit next to the person you've suggested), hold a buffet lunch instead. This will mean that people can mingle freely. On the other hand, if people who previously have

not got on well have started to thaw towards each other before lunch, you could act as a 'bridge' during the break and get them talking to each other outside the meeting venue too.

Step three: Keep on track

1 Start as you mean to go on

On the day of the meeting, arrive early so that you can check that everything is ready. Once the attendees are there, set the pace and tone of the meeting:

- ✔ Begin on time.
- ✔ Welcome everyone, and briefly explain basic issues such as where the toilets are located (particularly helpful for anyone who hasn't been to your offices before) and what the catering arrangements are.
- ✔ Ask everyone to check that they've turned off their mobile phones so that the flow of discussion isn't interrupted.
- ✔ Reiterate the reason the meeting is being held, what you hope to achieve within the meeting, the time-scale, and finishing time.

2 Keep a tight rein on proceedings

While obviously you need to give everyone an opportunity to contribute to points raised on the agenda, there are steps you can take to make sure that you keep roughly on schedule (and on topic).

- ✔ Make sure that attendees keep to one agenda point at a time.
- ✔ Firmly but politely move the discussion on if tempers start to flare.
- ✔ Don't let one person dominate the conversation. Meetings can often be hijacked by one or two vociferous attendees, so you need to make sure that everyone has a fair say.

Strategies for dealing with difficult people

The overly talkative: In the case of people who just like the sound of their own voice, you must be assertive enough to interject politely but firmly and remind everyone of the agenda point you're discussing and steer the discussion back to it. Also mention your target finish time and how the meeting is progressing in relation to it.

The passionate: The same goes for dealing with people who feel very strongly about the issue under discussion and who may feel that others do not share their interest and commitment. Again, make sure that they get the opportunity to voice their point of view, but also that they give others the chance to express theirs too. Interject as appropriate and summarise if you sense they are about to repeat something. Remember that a meeting is not an opportunity for attendees to rehearse an extended monologue.

The angry: If the topic you are discussing is particularly contentious, tempers may flare. If you feel a situation is getting heated and that insults rather than well-considered opinions are being traded, step in to defuse the tension. Suggest a break outside the meeting room for 15 minutes or so, which will give most people time to calm down and assess what has happened. If voices are being raised, match your voice to the level of other people's, then reduce the volume back down to a normal speaking pitch. This will allow the discussion to get back to a more stable footing.

The troublemakers: Some people are nightmares to work with. They may feel threatened by others, so try to hide their feelings of inadequacy by scoring cheap points or by trying to pick holes in *how* they say things rather than *what* they're saying (quibbling about choices of words, for example). Troublemakers may try to use meetings as a forum for raising gripes old and new, so you need to prepare yourself for dealing with these. Do your research so that you can use hard facts to put down 'throwaway' comments that the troublemaker may launch at you. Make sure that you appear to be impartial (however furious you may feel inside), and flush out trouble-making behaviour as early as you can. Be assertive and people will soon become tired of trying to cause a pointless rumpus.

✔ Make sure that there is only one discussion at a time. Meetings often get sidetracked when some attendees start their own 'private' meeting during the main session. This may range from a few whispered asides, to notes being passed around the table, to a full-blown separate discussion taking place. You'll never finish the main meeting on time if you allow that to happen, so take the initiative to stop these diversions by directly addressing the people involved and asking them if there's something they'd like to raise. For example, you could say: 'I think there may be an issue you're not happy with. Would you like to raise it now before we go any further? We have a lot to get through today.' Be assertive, not aggressive, polite but firm.

✔ Summarise at appropriate intervals and clearly restate agreed actionpoints.

Common mistakes

✗ You don't prepare properly

Meetings can be a terrible chore, but if you know you'll be chairing or participating in a potentially fraught meeting, it's well worth preparing yourself properly. Make sure you are up to speed with all relevant points so that you can answer quibbles with useful facts. If you know that some of the meeting's attendees just don't get on, think carefully about logistics, such as seating plans during the meeting and during lunch (if you're offering it). These may seem like small details, but looking after them really may make the difference between a meeting that is productive in spite of moments of tension, and a full-scale row.

✗ You don't tackle troublemakers

It's very important that, in your role as chair of the meeting, you defuse potentially explosive situations. If one person (or a group of people) is not letting anyone else participate properly, making snide or inappropriate comments, or just trying to hamper the meeting's proceedings so that you can't achieve your goals, you need to act. Call a halt to the meeting for a moment while you tackle those responsible politely but assertively, and ask them if they have a point they'd like to raise formally. Reiterate your schedule and the meeting's objectives, and make clear that their contribution isn't welcome in its current form. If you need to, call a break of ten minutes or so to let everyone cool down, then move on.

STEPS TO SUCCESS

- ✔ Only call a meeting if you think one is absolutely necessary.
- ✔ If a meeting does need to be called, give all attendees as much notice as you can.
- ✔ Take time to prepare yourself properly and look over the meeting objectives in advance.

- ✔ Make sure only one discussion is happening at any one time in the room.
- ✔ Give everyone an opportunity to get his or her point across and don't let the conversation be 'hijacked' by one person.

Useful links

Meeting Management Tips:
http://users.anytimenow.com/brian/meeting_management_tips.pdf
Meeting Wizard:
www.meetingwizard.org

Where to find more help

How to Work for an Idiot: Survive and Thrive . . . without Killing Your Boss

John Hoover

Career Press, 2003

256pp ISBN: 1564147045

Written by a self-confessed and recovering former idiot boss, this book is a guide for the down-trodden at work. It distinguishes between idiots and other types of toxic employers and offers practical solutions for how to cope with them, such as setting boundaries.

I Don't Know What I Want, But I Know It's Not This: A Step-by-step Guide to Finding Gratifying Work

Julie Jansen

London: Piatkus, 2004

270pp ISBN: 0273675826

If you've had enough of your current workplace or career but aren't sure where to turn for help, this book is an excellent first port of call. Full of exercises to assess the reader's personality and skills, this book will help people to understand their present situation and come up with ways to find the job or career they really want to embark on.

The Ultimate Guide to Successful Networking

Carole Stone

London: Vermilion 2004

176pp ISBN: 0091900255

This book is a guide to communicating more effectively in all areas of life so that confidence increases and new contacts can be made. Tapping into social networks is an excellent way to keep abreast of politicking in the workplace, and this is a useful skill to cultivate. The author overcame her own childhood shyness to become a successful radio producer.